Back to the Trees

by Tim Little
Illustrated by Claire Lefevre

Contents

OXFORD

UNIVERSITY PRESS

Orangutans under Threat

Orangutans live in the **rainforests** of Southeast Asia. Large areas of these rainforests are being cut down or burned. Things are looking <u>desperate</u> for the orangutans.

Luckily, there are specially trained people who help to look after orangutans that are lost or injured. They <u>provide</u> food and shelter for the orangutans.

The orangutans' situation is <u>desperate</u>. Does that mean it is very bad or that it is a bit difficult?

This little one is lost. She needs help so she can go back to the forest.

Who might <u>provide</u> food and shelter for this little orangutan until she's ready to go back to the rainforest?

Food and Drink

I need to drink lots of milk so I can get bigger.

Unusual means strange or not normal. What can you see in the picture that might be unusual for orangutans in the wild?

Human Helpers

The human helpers look after the baby orangutans like orangutan mums would in the **wild**. This is because it is very important for the baby **apes** to feel safe and cared for.

As they grow up, the orangutans are <u>introduced</u> to other orangutans, so that they can learn important skills from them.

Have you been <u>introduced</u> to someone, for example a new child at school? What did you say or do?

Tree Skills

I lift my arms up to swing in the trees!

Now I can look for food high up.

crunch crunch

9

Returning to the Wild

When the orangutans get a bit older, they spend less time with the human helpers and begin to live on their own.

The helpers watch the orangutans carefully and make a <u>decision</u> about when they can be returned to the wild. Then the orangutans will be free.

A <u>decision</u> is when you choose something or decide to do something. What was the last <u>decision</u> you made?

child

The helpers pick the best
spot to set her free.

Look at the trees! I can swing across the forest.

Free in the Wild

Once the orangutans are returned to the forest, they are kept far <u>apart</u> from humans. They can finally put all of the skills they have learned into practice. They are animals in the wild once again.

Orangutans are kept <u>apart</u> from humans. Can you move so that we are far <u>apart</u>?

Now I can get food, drink and shelter in the forest. I do not need help!

Glossary

apes: animals like large monkeys with long arms and no tail

rainforests: thick forests in warm parts of the world where a lot of rain falls

shelter: a place that protects people or animals from bad weather or danger

wild: the places where animals and plants live without humans

Index

Throughout the book there are words in **bold**. We can use the Glossary together to look up what these words mean. The Index will help us find key information.